HEAT, LIGHTS AND ACTION!

HOW ELECTRICITY WORKS

EVE & ALBERT STWERTKA
PICTURES BY MENA DOLOBOWSKY

JULIAN ⓜ MESSNER

JULIAN MESSNER and colophon are trademarks of Simon & Schuster, Inc.

Design by Malle N. Whitaker.
Manufactured in the United States of America.

Lib. ed.
10 9 8 7 6 5 4 3 2 1
Paper ed.
10 9 8 7 6 5 4 3 2 1

Library of Congress Cataloging-in-Publication Data
Stwertka, Eve.
     Heat, lights and action! : How electricity works / Eve and Albert Stwertka.
          p.   cm. — (At home with science)
     Includes index.
     Summary: Shows how energy in the form of electricity does a variety of tasks in and around the home. Readers learn to conduct their own experiments in making electricity.
     1. Electricity—Juvenile literature.   2. Force and energy—Juvenile literature.
     [1. Electricity.]   I. Stwertka, Albert.   II. Title.   III. Series.
     QC527.2.S79 1991   90-49109
     537—dc20   CIP AC
     ISBN 0-671-69458-8 (LSB)
     ISBN 0-671-69464-2 (pbk.)

CONTENTS

ENERGY

What's going on here? Lights are blazing. The doorbell is ringing. A snappy tune bursts from the radio. In the kitchen, a timer buzzes. The toast pops up out of the toaster. The blender sloshes pancake batter round and round.

It's just an ordinary winter morning. Breakfast is cooking. Soon your friend is coming to pick you up on the way to school. But what is this amazing power that rings bells and buzzers? What power turns beaters and makes the light bulbs blaze with light? It takes **energy** to do all this work!

5

Without energy, nothing can move or change. You need energy to play, walk your dog, even to read a book. You get this energy from the food you eat. But what about the energy that creates light and heat? What makes the machines work in your house? The answer is **electricity**.

But what is electricity? How is it made?

Electricity does many different jobs around your house. Can you write down what they are? Your list may turn out to be surprisingly long.

WHAT IS ELECTRICITY?

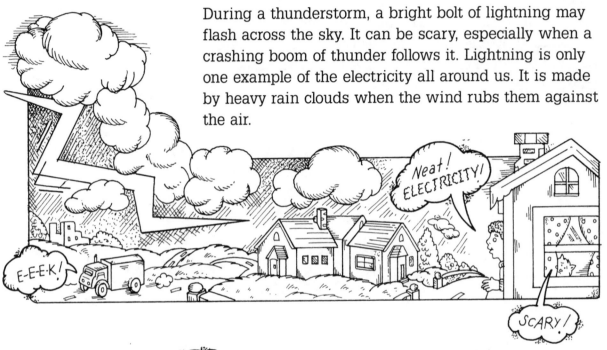

During a thunderstorm, a bright bolt of lightning may flash across the sky. It can be scary, especially when a crashing boom of thunder follows it. Lightning is only one example of the electricity all around us. It is made by heavy rain clouds when the wind rubs them against the air.

You can make your own electricity: Stand in front of a mirror in a dark room. Be sure there is a carpet under your feet. Then brush your hair briskly. Make sure your hair is dry. Can you see little flashes of light? Can you feel the sparks jumping?

Atoms and Electrical Charges

Everything in the world is made up of tiny bits of matter called **atoms**. Your body is made up of atoms. So are even very small things. A speck of dust is made up of billions and billions of atoms. Each atom is made up of even smaller parts. It has a tiny **nucleus** surrounded by **electrons** that revolve around it. These parts of the atom are held together by **electrical charges**.

Everything is made up of atoms! Even me!

We are all made up of BILLIONS of atoms!

Even the fish!?!

Us too!

YUP!

There are only two kinds of electrical charges. One is called positive, and the other negative. A positive charge and a negative charge always attract each other. In an atom, the nucleus is positively charged. The electrons are negatively charged. The attraction between them keeps the atom from flying apart.

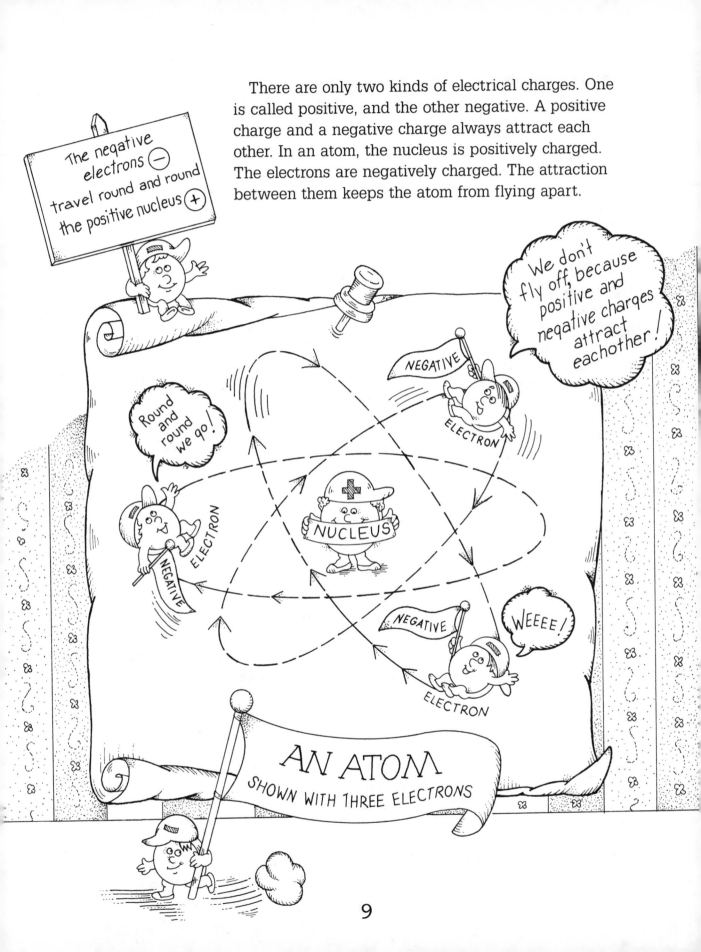

In some materials, though, the electrons are not very strongly attracted by the nucleus. In that case the electrons can easily be removed, even by rubbing.

Try this...

Scatter a few small pieces of paper on a table. Rub a plastic comb or ruler with a piece of wool cloth. Hold the comb over the paper. Can you see the bits of paper jumping up to the comb? Rubbing removes some of the electrons from the wool cloth. They then attach themselves to the comb. The comb now has too many electrons and an extra negative charge. This charge strongly attracts the positive charges in the paper.

WOOL CLOTH

PLASTIC COMB

BITS OF PAPER

AMAZING!

ZIP

ZIP!

Try the rubbing experiment with a metal spoon instead of a comb. Nothing happens because the spoon doesn't build up a charge. The electrons that are rubbed off the cloth flow through the spoon into your hand. Then they travel through your body into the ground.

Metal is a good **conductor** of electricity. This is because streams of electrons can easily flow through it. Plastic, on the other hand, is an **insulator**, or nonconductor of electricity. This is because electrons cannot easily move through it.

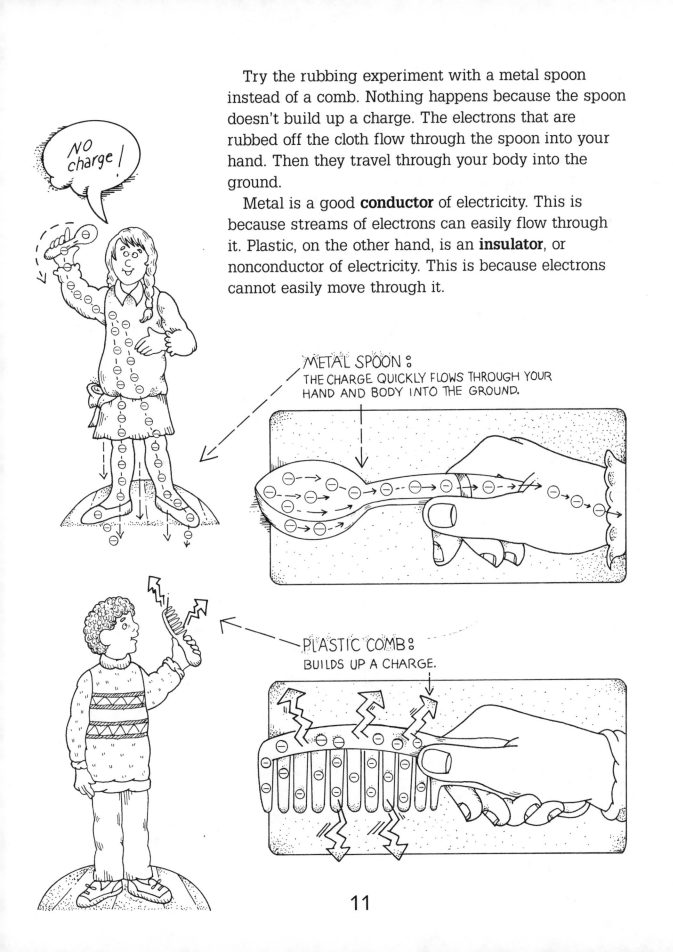

NO charge!

METAL SPOON:
THE CHARGE QUICKLY FLOWS THROUGH YOUR HAND AND BODY INTO THE GROUND.

PLASTIC COMB:
BUILDS UP A CHARGE.

Rubbing a spoon produces only a very short flow of electrons. To make enough electricity for a city, steady streams of electrons are needed. They must flow in a continuous **circuit**.

A circuit is a loop or circle in which electrons travel. They travel from a source of power and back again. The electrons flow most easily through metal wires. This is because metals are good conductors of electricity.

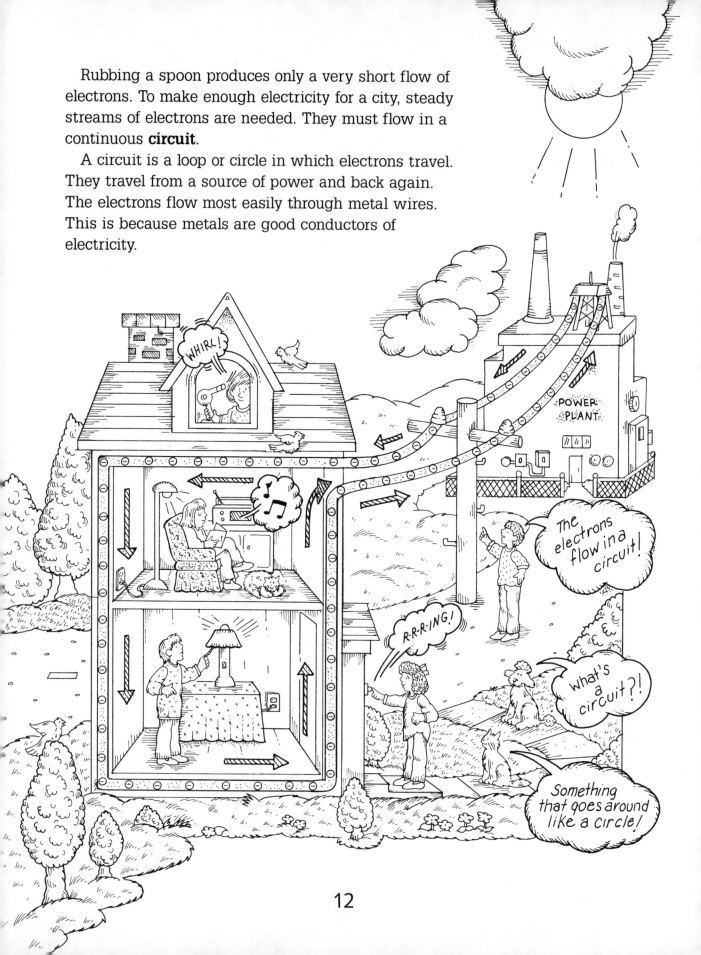

To keep moving around the circuit, electrons need a constant push. This push comes from a source of energy. The energy may come from a battery or a power station.

The pressure that pushes the electricity through the wire is measured in **volts**. The higher the voltage, the stronger the flow of electricity, and the more work it can do.

Try this...

Look at some of the appliances in your home. Be sure to unplug them first. Is there a voltage requirement marked on them? Notice that almost all of them need 120V, or 120 volts. This requirement is standard for most appliances in the United States.

Suppose we want the flow of electricity to stop. We have to interrupt the circuit. This is the job of the switches in your house. Turn off your light switch, for example. Two pieces of metal inside the switch separate. Now the electricity can't pass through the wire. Turn the switch on. The two pieces of metal join together again. The circuit is completed and you have light once more.

SWITCH IS OFF, CIRCUIT IS BROKEN. NO ELECTRONS CAN FLOW.

ELECTRONS →

SWITCH IS ON. A COMPLETE CIRCUIT MEANS ELECTRONS CAN FLOW.

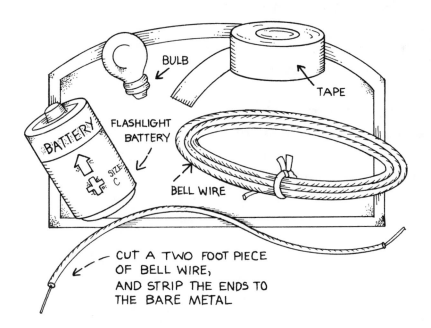

BULB

TAPE

FLASHLIGHT
BATTERY

BATTERY
SIZE
C

BELL WIRE

CUT A TWO FOOT PIECE
OF BELL WIRE,
AND STRIP THE ENDS TO
THE BARE METAL

Try this...

Get a flashlight battery, a flashlight bulb, and some wire. You can buy a 25-foot coil of "bell wire" in any hardware store. To light the bulb you need a complete circuit. Tape one end of the wire to the bottom of the battery. Wind the other end around the metal base of the bulb. Nothing happens.

Now touch the tip of the bulb to the top of the battery. You can tell that you have completed a circuit because the bulb lights up.

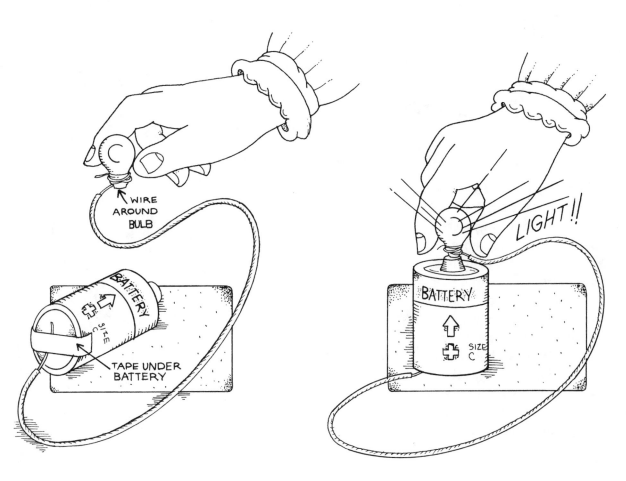

WIRE
AROUND
BULB

BATTERY
SIZE
C

TAPE UNDER
BATTERY

LIGHT!!

BATTERY
SIZE
C

The flow of electricity in a metal is actually very uneven. The electrons are constantly bumping into atoms that get in their way. With each bump they slow down and lose energy. This is called **electrical resistance.**

The longer and narrower the wire, the greater the resistance. The greater the resistance, the more energy is lost. The power station has to work constantly to replace this lost energy and keep the electrons moving.

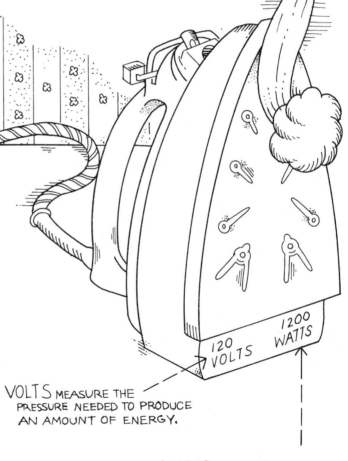

Try this...

Some appliances use a lot of energy in a short time. The amount of energy used per second is measured in *watts.* A 150-watt bulb uses more energy per second than a 75-watt bulb. More energy makes the bulb give off more heat and light. This explains why the 150-watt bulb is brighter than the 75-watt bulb. Examine some of the appliances in your home. How many watts do they use?

120 VOLTS

1200 WATTS

VOLTS MEASURE THE PRESSURE NEEDED TO PRODUCE AN AMOUNT OF ENERGY.

WATTS MEASURE THE ENERGY THE APPLIANCE USES PER SECOND.

16

Electricity and Magnets

An amazing thing happens when electricity flows through a coil of wire. The coil becomes a **magnet**, which attracts metals. It can also make metal objects move so that they can ring bells or drive motors.

   This change works the other way around too. Any movement of a magnet near a wire will produce electricity. In fact, that's how the power company makes electricity.

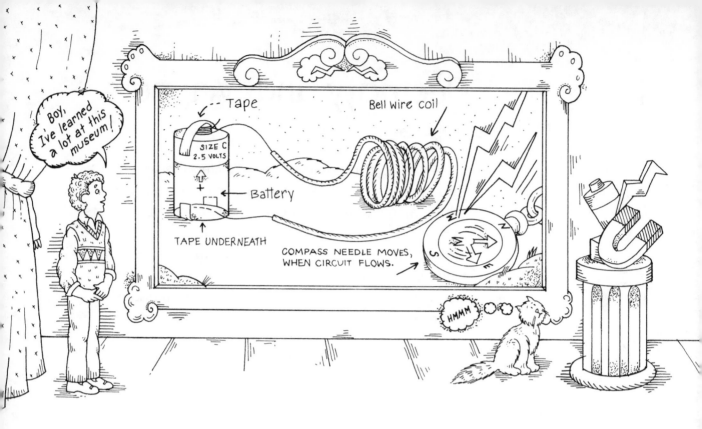

Tape

Bell wire coil

SIZE C
2.5 VOLTS

Battery

TAPE UNDERNEATH

COMPASS NEEDLE MOVES,
WHEN CIRCUIT FLOWS.

Boy,
I've learned
a lot at this
museum!

HMMM

Try this...

Take a 25-foot coil of bell wire and remove about an inch of the plastic covering from both ends. Tape one end to the bottom of a flashlight battery, and tape the other end to the top. This forms a circuit. Now place a compass near the wire coil. Watch the compass needle move as the coil becomes magnetic.

Now remove the battery. Wrap one end of the wire around a compass. Make several turns. Twist the two bare wire ends together. Pass a bar magnet back and forth inside the wire coil. Watch the compass needle move. The moving magnet is producing electricity.

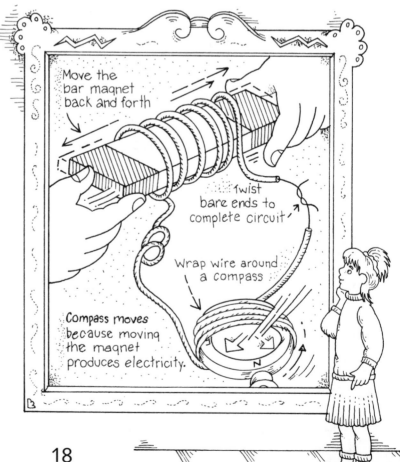

Move the bar magnet back and forth

Twist bare ends to complete circuit

Wrap wire around a compass

Compass moves because moving the magnet produces electricity.

FROM POWERHOUSE TO YOUR HOUSE

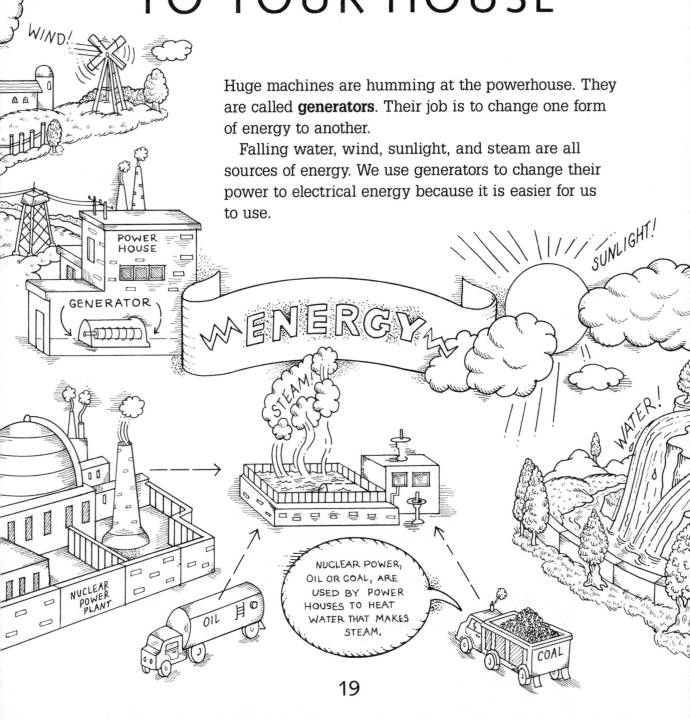

Huge machines are humming at the powerhouse. They are called **generators**. Their job is to change one form of energy to another.

Falling water, wind, sunlight, and steam are all sources of energy. We use generators to change their power to electrical energy because it is easier for us to use.

WIND!

POWER HOUSE

GENERATOR

ENERGY

SUNLIGHT!

STEAM

WATER!

NUCLEAR POWER PLANT

OIL

NUCLEAR POWER, OIL OR COAL, ARE USED BY POWER HOUSES TO HEAT WATER THAT MAKES STEAM.

COAL

19

Inside each generator are coils of wire. These coils surround a magnetic core that is spinning very fast. The force needed to spin this magnet often comes from steam. To make steam, power plants heat thousands of gallons of water. Some heat the water by burning coal. Others use oil. Still others use nuclear power.

As the magnet spins, electricity starts to flow through the surrounding coils. From the coils it travels to the outside world through bundles of wires. These are called cables.

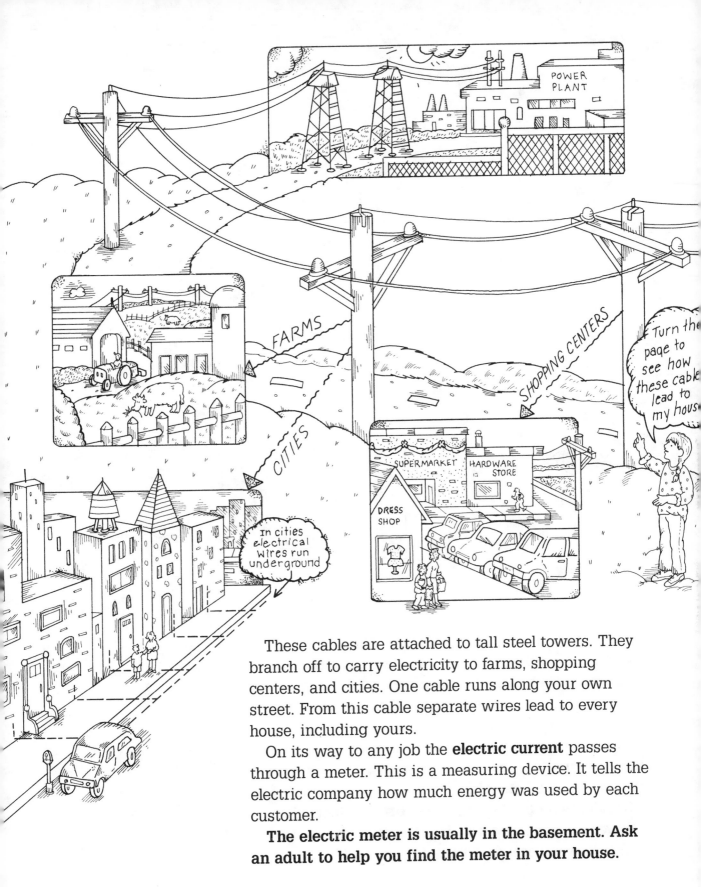

These cables are attached to tall steel towers. They branch off to carry electricity to farms, shopping centers, and cities. One cable runs along your own street. From this cable separate wires lead to every house, including yours.

On its way to any job the **electric current** passes through a meter. This is a measuring device. It tells the electric company how much energy was used by each customer.

The electric meter is usually in the basement. Ask an adult to help you find the meter in your house.

21

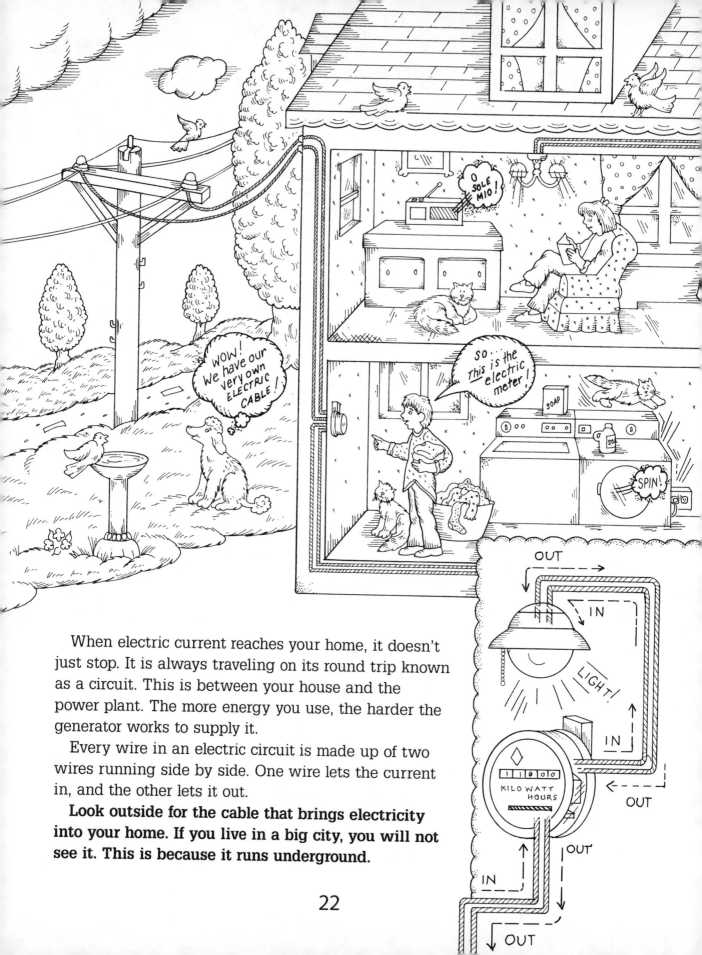

When electric current reaches your home, it doesn't just stop. It is always traveling on its round trip known as a circuit. This is between your house and the power plant. The more energy you use, the harder the generator works to supply it.

Every wire in an electric circuit is made up of two wires running side by side. One wire lets the current in, and the other lets it out.

Look outside for the cable that brings electricity into your home. If you live in a big city, you will not see it. This is because it runs underground.

22

The wires that carry electricity through your home are hidden inside the walls. You can plug into the electric current through outlets and sockets. These are placed in convenient spots around the rooms.

Remember, electric wires are made of two parts. That's why outlets need two openings and plugs need two prongs. Just plug in the wire of a lamp or machine. Then flick the switch, or push the button, that completes the circuit. There it goes! Your appliance is working!

23

ENERGY GOES TO WORK

Each appliance in your home takes as much electricity as it needs. Then it changes it to a different form of energy. Some appliances produce heat energy. Others produce light energy. Still others produce energy of motion, or mechanical energy.

Heat!

Take a look at your toaster oven, for example. Toasters are designed to change electric energy into heat energy.

Hungry for a toasted muffin? Put your muffin on the toaster tray. Set the timer. Inside, a switch closes to complete the electric circuit. Electric current starts to flow. The electrons in the wire dance and jiggle. They try to pass through the heating coil inside the toaster.

Care to dance?!

IT'S fun to be an ELECTRON!

the electric current flows, and we electrons really get going!

HOT!

HEATING COIL ---

The heating coil is made of a special kind of metal. It keeps the electrons from passing through the coil easily. This resistance causes the electrons to bump and push against the atoms. They act like a big crowd of people trying to go through a small gate. The electrons jostle the atoms so hard that the metal of the heating coil gets very hot.

Another word for rubbing is **friction**. Rub your hands together briskly to feel how friction produces heat. Your skin gets hot because the electrons and atoms are being pushed and prodded.

When the toaster coil heats up, the metal glows with a red light. Light and heat energy often appear together. Think of a campfire. It's both hot and bright.

To help you heat your food just right, the toaster oven has a built-in timer. When the time you set has gone by, a switch opens to break the circuit. The heating stops. Your muffin is ready!

Light!

Toasters give off some light. But their main job is to make heat. Light bulbs also give off heat. But their main job is to produce light.

When you switch on a lamp, electric current flows through the bulb. It passes through a wire as thin as a hair. This wire is called the **filament**. In the narrow filament, the electrons crowd and jostle the atoms so hard that they heat up the wire.

Look for the filament in a light bulb made of clear glass. But first turn off the light so it can't hurt your eyes.

FILAMENT - ENLARGED

← FILAMENT

I don't work any more, but my filament glowed just like this once!

INSIDE THE FILAMENT, THE ELECTRONS TRY TO MOVE FORWARD, BUT THE ATOMS CAUSE THEM TO SWERVE AND BOUNCE OFF IN ALL DIRECTIONS.

— ELECTRONS

ATOMS

The filament is blazing hot. But it can't burn. This is because there is no air inside the bulb. Nothing can burn without air. The filament can't melt because its special metal is too tough. Instead, it starts to glow very brightly, giving off brilliant white light.

Which appliances in your house change energy mainly to heat? Which ones change it mainly to light?

Action!

The job of many household appliances is to move or turn things. Cake mixers, fans, washers, and other machines are very much alike. They all use a motor to change electrical energy to mechanical energy. Mechanical energy is the energy of motion.

Inside a motor, two magnets face each other. Between them rests a core of coiled magnetic wire. This core can turn over freely. When electricity passes through the motor, magnetic forces act on the wire core. They push it, pull it, turn it over, and make it spin.

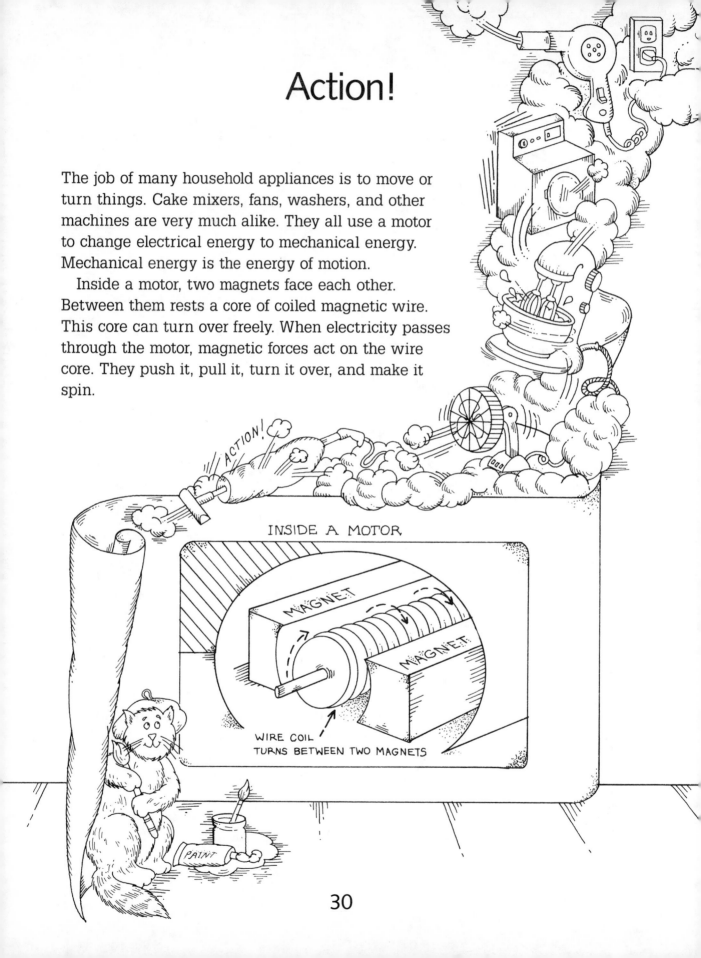

INSIDE A MOTOR

MAGNET

MAGNET

WIRE COIL
TURNS BETWEEN TWO MAGNETS

30

The turning core of the motor is used to turn other parts of the machine. It works in much the way your feet do when you ride a bike. Your feet push the pedals to make the bike's wheels turn.

Motors do small jobs and big jobs. They turn fans like those that suck air into vacuum cleaners. They spin the drum of your laundry dryer. They also wind and unwind the heavy cables in elevators. These cables pull elevators filled with people to the top of a building. Then they let them down again.

GUARDING THE DRAGON

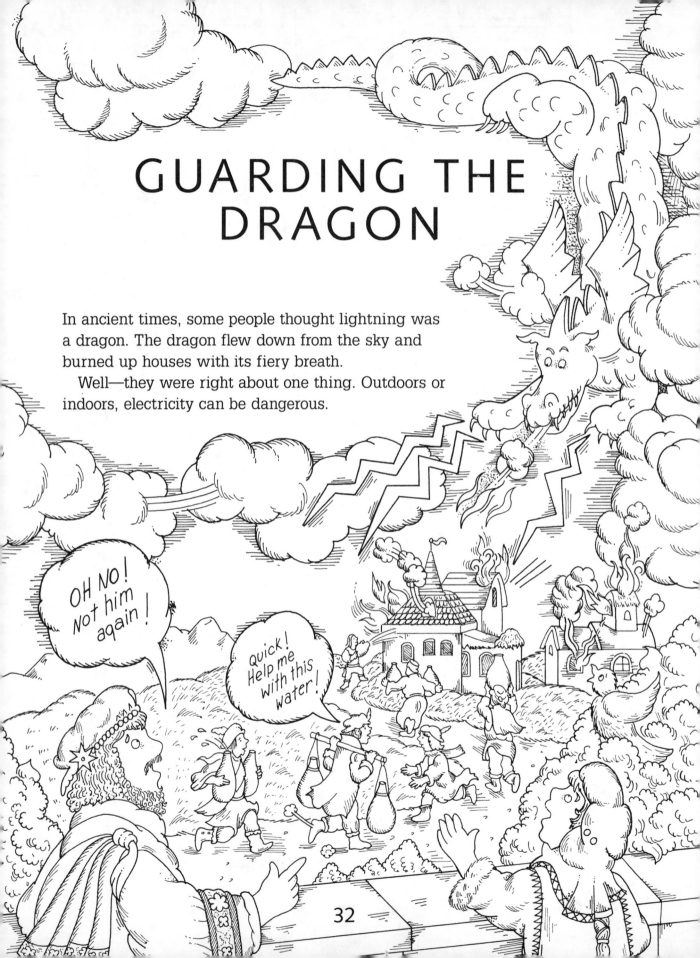

In ancient times, some people thought lightning was a dragon. The dragon flew down from the sky and burned up houses with its fiery breath.

Well—they were right about one thing. Outdoors or indoors, electricity can be dangerous.

OH NO! Not him again!

Quick! Help me with this water!

You may wonder why electric current never escapes through the outlets in your wall. What keeps it from darting into your room like a bolt of lightning? The answer is that electricity travels only through materials that are good conductors. Metal wire is a good conductor, but air is a very poor conductor. Electricity travels through air only when it has no wire to go through and no other way to reach the ground.

But the human body is a better conductor than air. If you accidentally touched electric current, it would travel right through your body and disappear into the earth. This would be a terrible shock to your system.

A shock of strong electric current can paralyze a person's nervous system. It can prevent the person from breathing. It can even stop the heart from beating.

Water, too, is a better conductor than air. That's why it's very dangerous to take an ordinary radio into the bathroom with you. Touching it with wet hands or dropping it into the bathtub sets up a pathway for an electric current to pass through your body.

34

The electrical parts of appliances are insulated by a protective covering. This prevents electric current from giving people shocks or starting fires. Insulation is made of special materials that are poor electrical conductors. Rubber and plastic are such materials.

All wires, cables, cords, plugs, and sockets are insulated. Never use a broken cord, plug, or appliance. You might receive an electric shock.

35

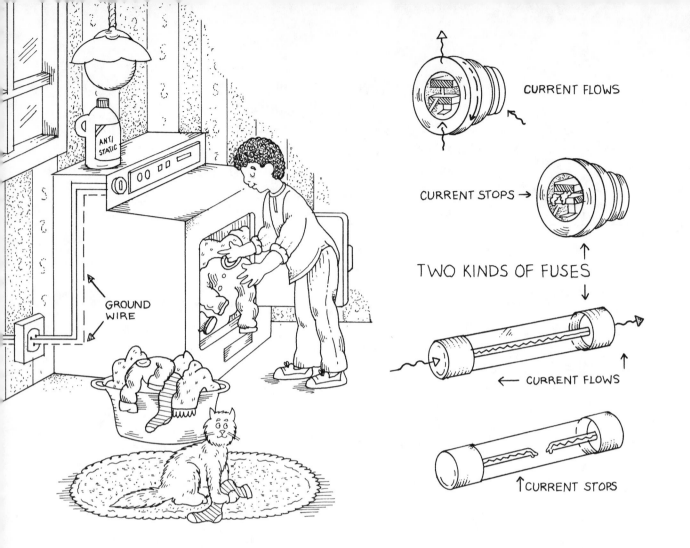

CURRENT FLOWS

CURRENT STOPS →

TWO KINDS OF FUSES

← CURRENT FLOWS

↑CURRENT STOPS

GROUND WIRE

Some plugs and appliances carry a ground wire for safety. If the appliance is broken the ground wire provides a way for the electric current to flow safely into the ground.

Every electrical circuit is equipped with a safety fuse or a circuit breaker. A fuse is a thin wire that forms part of the circuit. If too much current flows through the system, the fuse melts. The circuit is broken. The electricity stops.

A circuit breaker works more like a switch. When too much current flows, it opens. This breaks the circuit and no more current can flow.

The box where all fuses or circuit breakers come together is likely to be in the basement or hallway of your house. Ask an adult to help you find it.

This is the circuit breaker

Today we know that electricity is not a dragon. Instead it is a powerful natural force. It can help us in many wonderful ways. But we have to guard it and use it with care.

37

GLOSSARY

Atom—The smallest unit of any kind of matter. Atoms are the building blocks of matter.

Circuit (SUR-kit)—The complete path, in a loop or circle, of an electric current.

Conductor (Ken-DUK-ter)—Any material through which electric current can pass easily. Copper wire is a conductor of electricity.

Electrical charge (e-LEK-tri-kel charj)—Any given quantity of electricity.

Electrical resistance (e-LEK-tri-kel ri-ZIS-tens)—Anything that prevents electricity from flowing easily through a material.

Electric current (e-LEK-tri-kel KUR-ent)—The flow of electricity through a wire.

Electricity (e-LEK-tris-i-te)—A general term to describe either electric current or the effects caused by the presence of too many electrons.

Electron (e-LEK-tron)—One of the basic particles that make up an atom. The movement of electrons through a wire is called electric current.

Energy—The ability to do work.

Filament (FIL-e-ment)—A thin wire that gives off light when heated to a high temperature.

Friction (FRIK-shen)—The rubbing of one material against another. Friction produces heat.

Fuse—A safety device used to prevent electric circuits from overloading.

Generator (JEN-e-ra-ter)—A device that changes mechanical energy, energy of motion, into electrical energy.

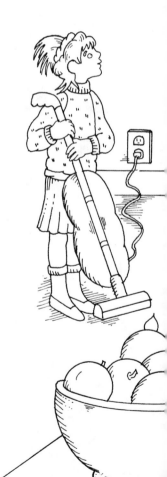

Insulator (IN-se-la-ter)—Any material that is a poor conductor of electricity. Plastic is an insulator, or nonconductor, of electricity.

Magnet—Any natural iron ore that can attract other pieces of iron or steel.

Nucleus (NOO-kle-es)—The center of an atom.

Volt—A unit that measures the pressure that pushes electric current through a wire.

Watt—A unit that measures the amount of electrical energy used per second by an appliance.

INDEX